AF504384

What Do
You Do
with
Your Poo?

By Courtney Ball

Illustrated by Lana Hadziosmanovic

UnRote Press
Cedar Rapids, IA, USA

For my girls.

Copyright © 2024 by Courtney Ball

All rights reserved.

No portion of this book may be reproduced in any form without written permission from the publisher or author, except as permitted by U.S. copyright law.

Cover and Illustrations by Lana Hadziosmanovic

Published by UnRote Press
Cedar Rapids, IA, USA
First printing June of 2024

ISBN 979-8-218-42398-8

FROM
FOOD
TO
POOED

You poo.
Of course you do.
But once you poo,
then what do you do?

A bunny rabbit eats her own poo.
Hamsters, guinea pigs, and rats do too.

What about you?
Is that what you do?

Would you put it in your stew
or use it for fondue?

Well, you can decide.
It belongs to you.
Unless you're like the two-toed sloth
way down in Peru
who (s-l-o-w-l-y) sneaks around
and steals others' poo.

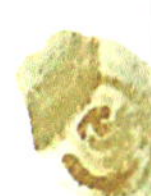

YOU GONNA
EAT THAT?

Now, a dog or a hog
may eat its own pile.
or snack on another's
every once in a while.

Poop is a thing most people find vile.
What about you?
Does poop make you smile?

So many animals eat poop!
I can't name them all.
Most of them are tiny,
little bugs that creep and crawl,
like the feisty dung beetle
who rolls it up in a ball.

Not all of them are little.
Go to the zoo, and you'll see.
Even the mighty gorilla
or the tricky chimpanzee.

They both like to eat poo
But don't get too close,
or they'll throw it at you!

What about you
do you ever throw poo?

To eat a friend's poo is one thing
but here is quite another.
A baby koala bear
eats poop from its mother.

Blech! That's so gross it makes me moan.
But guess what;
baby koalas aren't alone.

PROBIOTICS

Say you meet an elephant
or a young hippo from Nigeria.
They also eat their mothers' poop
to get the right bacteria.

If they didn't do that
they couldn't digest their food.
I bet you're glad you don't have to eat
the stuff that your mom pooed.

And speaking of hippos...

When a hippo goes poop
she'll swish her short tail like a fan,
She shakes it fast to fling her poo
as far as she possibly can.

Not every animal at the zoo
can fling it like the hippos do,
but if you stood behind a penguin,
they might squirt it on your shoe.

Some penguins shoot it out
like a little butt gun.
You probably can't do that
but do you think it sounds fun?

SURE IS HOT
TODAY...

Vultures can live in hot, hot places
where they might not have a pool.
They sometimes poop and pee on their legs
to help themselves keep cool.

What about you?
Is this something you might try?
Or would you just let yourself fry?
Now, be honest. Please don't lie.

A fieldfare thrush lives in Europe
and seems like a harmless bird
but don't you dare threaten her babies,
or she'll bomb you with a turd.

I wonder, if you could fly
way up high in the sky
would it help you feel calm
if you could drop a poop bomb?

Or, maybe you don't like to throw your poo away.
You could keep it and use it some way.
If you were like a wombat
whose poop is shaped like a block
you could use it to build a house.
That would make the neighbors talk!

All these things you could do with your poo!
And most people just flush it down the loo.
That's kind of boring, don't you think?
But I guess then you get rid of the stink.

After I poop, I want it to go away!
But that's just me. 
Maybe you don't feel that way?

About the Author

Courtney Ball is a father, storyteller, community builder, film/video producer, and photographer. He and his wife Emmy live in Cedar Rapids, IA. This is by far the silliest thing he has written, and he enjoyed the process very much.

Learn more about him at CourtneyBall.com